Mr. Noisy

Mr. Noisy made noise when he walked.

Mr. Noisy made noise when he talked.

Mr. Noisy made noise when he danced.

Mr. Noisy made noise when he sang.

Mr. Noisy made noise when he drove his car.

Mr. Noisy made noise when he rode his bike.

"It's too noisy!" everybody yelled.

9

Mr. Noisy walked quietly.

Mr. Noisy talked quietly.

Mr. Noisy danced quietly.

Mr. Noisy sang quietly.
Mr. Noisy drove his car quietly.

Mr. Noisy rode his bike quietly.

"It's too quiet!" everybody yelled.
"Where's Mr. Noisy?"

"Here I am!"